Inspirational
AUTHORS

This journal belongs to

_____

Grow with Grace:

21 Days to YOUR Life in Bloom!

Phoenix Grace, BSW

Grow with Grace: 21 Days to YOUR Life in Bloom!

Published by ILLUMINATION PRESS
ATLANTA, GA

Copyright 2023 by Phoenix Grace, BSW. All rights reserved.

No part of this book may be reproduced in any form or by any mechanical means, including information storage and retrieval systems without permission in writing from the publisher/author, except by a reviewer who may quote passages in a review.

All images, logos, quotes, and trademarks included in this book are subject to use according to trademark and copyright laws of the United States of America.

ISBN: 978-1-950681-49-5

Unless otherwise indicated, all Scripture quotations are taken from the Holy Bible, New International Version®, NIV®. Copyright © 1973, 1978, 1984, 2011 by Biblica, Inc.™ Used by permission of Zondervan. All rights reserved worldwide. www.zondervan.com The "NIV" and "New International Version" are trademarks registered in the United States Patent and Trademark Office by Biblica, Inc.™

Interior design by August Pride, LLC
All rights reserved.
Printed in the United States of America.

ILLUMINATION PRESS
c/o Benecia Ponder
1100 Peachtree Street
Suite 250
Atlanta, GA 30309

Inspire@InspirationalAuthors.com
www.InspirationalAuthors.com

Acknowledgments

Butterfly cover art and butterfly journal page illustrations by Donna Hinett of **FlitsAndGiggles.com**

Floral doodles by Prawny, designer at **creativefabrica.com**

HELLO Beautiful
WOMAN OF GOD

Welcome to YOUR Life in Bloom!

What is "Life in Bloom"?

Life in Bloom is:
- ABUNDANT LIFE
- Wholeness
- Restoration
- Freedom
- Empowerment
- Authenticity
- Connection (to God, self, and others)
- Balance/wellness in all areas of life: physical, mental, emotional, spiritual

Life in Bloom! is what God intended for creation. Adam and Eve lived the fullness and richness of life in the garden. There was no sickness or disease, their needs were provided for, and they were intimately connected to God. Then came the serpent, the fruit from the wrong tree, and the fall from grace.

We are new creations and have been made righteous in Christ. But, many times, as women, we do not step fully into our birthright as daughters of the king.

We get stuck in the PAST, in our EMOTIONS, in our CIRCUMSTANCES or in OLD WAYS of doing things that drain our vitality and vibrancy. Our spirits are born again but the thief of our soul has made it his mission to steal, kill and destroy all that belongs to God, including our peace, our health, and our destinies.

Journey from Pain to Promise
From Striving to Thriving
(Phoenix Grace's story)

> "You have walked through fire and survived; now you will rise from the ashes and thrive"

Walking through fire…

I have been through fire both literally (third degree burns from the waist up) and figuratively (father died when I was six, married/divorced twice, etc.) For many years, I lived life way (way) out of bloom.

I tried to fill (what I later found out was) the God-shaped hole in my life with all the things of the world. I tried religion (new age/wicca/ reiki, liberal Christianity and even Zen Buddhism), relationships (you name it), and education/career (received a Bachelor of Social Work degree and 3/4 of a Master of Social Work degree).

I tried being good and then I tried being bad. I found out all the things that didn't work. Then, in the middle of a long wilderness season, I quit trying so hard. I let go and let God in. I came to Christ.

Rising from Ashes...

Fast forward several years, and I am now a sold out, all in, spirit-filled believer. God has given me a new name (literally- "Phoenix Grace" comes from the Word I heard when I woke up from a dream) and a new story for my life.

He has taught me balance and he is restoring me- body, soul, and spirit.

Thriving (and helping others to thrive..)

I am so grateful and blessed for my second chance at life. I have made it my mission to stop the enemy in his attempt to steal, kill, and destroy our bodies, souls, and spirits. I do not want to see anyone live in that place of physical, mental/emotional and spiritual stagnation and overwhelm that I experienced when so much more is available!

I am passionate about helping to empower other women like YOU to be who they were CREATED to be and go from surviving to thriving in all aspects of life.

As I reflect on my own journey of transformation, I want you to know that my story is not just about my past but a testament to the hope that resides in all of us.

Through Christ, we find the strength to rise from our ashes, no matter how dire our circumstances may seem. The trials and tribulations I've faced only serve as a testament to the power of faith, resilience, and God's unwavering love.

My life is proof that with His grace, all things are possible, and true, lasting transformation can be achieved. My deepest desire is for you to discover that same transformative power within you.

You too can rise, thrive, and flourish, as we embark on this shared path of growth, healing, and spiritual renewal.

Now, let's embark on this transformative journey together!

"Grow With Grace: 21 Days to YOUR Life in Bloom!" is a journey of self-discovery, personal growth, and spiritual transformation. The pages within this book will help you nurture your spiritual, physical, mental, and emotional health.

How the Book is Organized

Week 1: Prepare the Soil: Cultivating Your Authentic Self focuses on preparing the soil for personal growth and spiritual development. It encourages reflection, taking a holistic approach to wellness, and cultivating authenticity. We'll explore how to nourish your body as a temple, renew your mind, clear emotional clutter, plant seeds of spiritual growth, establish a healthy routine, grow in emotional intelligence, and foster authentic faith connections.

It's the foundation upon which you'll build the beautiful garden of your soul.

Week 2: Planting Seeds of Connection: Nurturing Relationships will take you on a journey that delves into using your unique gifts and talents to serve, embracing a growth mindset, nurturing relationships with love and kindness, tending to emotional well-being, watering your faith through prayer and worship, and growing in wisdom and knowledge while cultivating gratitude.

You'll learn how to deepen your connections with others and flourish in the garden of relationships.

Week 3: Opening the Garden Gate: Establishing Boundaries for Growth will empower you to embrace vulnerability, set healthy boundaries, practice mindfulness, release control, cultivate joy and creativity, practice forgiveness, and step into the freedom found in Christ.

This is where your journey will culminate, leading you toward personal growth and spiritual transformation.

Each day, we will delve into the wisdom of scriptures, contemplate thought-provoking journal prompts, and be empowered by declarations that will guide you on your path to a life in full bloom.

So, my dear sister, I encourage you to open your heart and mind to the pages ahead. Be prepared for moments of insight, growth, and, most importantly, a deeper connection with our Heavenly Father.

May this journey be a blessing, an inspiration, and a source of unshakable faith. Embrace it with an open heart, and watch as your life flourishes in grace, wisdom, and love.

Keep Bloomin' in Him,

Phoenix Grace

The thief does not come except to
steal, and to kill, and to destroy.
I have come that they may have
LIFE, and that they may have it
more abundantly.
John 10:10 (NKJV)

WEEK 1
Prepare the Soil:
Cultivating Your Authentic Self

"The glory of gardening: hands in the dirt, head in the sun, heart with nature. To nurture a garden is to feed not just the body, but the soul."

Alfred Austin

Nourish temple, heart, and soul.
Clear emotions, spirit's seed,
In routines thrive, faith takes lead.
Embrace intelligence's art,
Week one's journey; faith's fresh start.

DAY 1
Nourishing Your Temple

"Do you not know that your bodies are temples of the Holy Spirit, who is in you, whom you have received from God? You are not your own; you were bought at a price. Therefore honor God with your bodies."

1 Corinthians 6:19-20 (NIV)

Reflect on the importance of taking care of your physical body as a temple of the Holy Spirit.

How can you honor God by nourishing your body with whole foods and engaging in regular exercise?

_____
_____
_____
_____
_____
_____
_____
_____
_____
_____
_____
_____
_____
_____
_____
_____
_____

Consider how your physical well-being impacts your mental, emotional, and spiritual health.

How can you prioritize self-care practices that promote overall wellness?

_____
_____
_____
_____
_____
_____
_____
_____
_____
_____
_____
_____
_____
_____
_____
_____

Declaration

"I declare that my body is a temple of the Holy Spirit, and I will honor God by nourishing it with whole foods and engaging in regular exercise. I choose to glorify God in my body and prioritize my physical well-being, knowing that it impacts my mental, emotional, and spiritual health."

DAY 2

Cultivating a Renewed Mind

"Do not conform to the pattern of this world, but be transformed by the renewing of your mind. Then you will be able to test and approve what God's will is—his good, pleasing and perfect will."

Romans 12:2 (NIV)

Reflect on the power of renewing your mind with God's truth. How can you fill your mind with Scripture and positive, uplifting thoughts that align with God's Word?

Identify one negative thought pattern or self-limiting belief you want to uproot.

How can you replace it with God's promises and cultivate a mindset of faith and hope?

_____
_____
_____
_____
_____
_____
_____
_____
_____
_____
_____
_____
_____
_____

DAY 3

Clearing Emotional Clutter

"Cast all your anxiety on him because he cares for you."

1 Peter 5:7 (NIV)

Take inventory of any unresolved emotions or emotional baggage that may hinder your well-being.

How can you surrender these burdens to God and seek His healing and restoration?

_____
_____
_____
_____
_____
_____
_____
_____
_____
_____
_____
_____
_____
_____
_____
_____
_____
_____

Reflect on the importance of forgiveness, both toward others and yourself.

How can you release any bitterness or resentment and cultivate a heart of grace and mercy?

_____
_____
_____
_____
_____
_____
_____
_____
_____
_____
_____
_____
_____
_____
_____
_____
_____

Declaration:

"I declare that I will surrender any unresolved emotions or emotional baggage to God. I seek His healing and restoration in my life. I choose to release bitterness and resentment, embracing forgiveness toward others and myself. I cultivate a heart of grace and mercy, allowing God to clear away emotional clutter."

DAY 4

Planting Seeds of Spiritual Growth

"But grow in the grace and knowledge of our Lord and Savior Jesus Christ. To him be glory both now and forever! Amen."

2 Peter 3:18 (NIV)

Reflect on your spiritual journey and the areas in which you desire to grow closer to God.

How can you deepen your prayer life, engage in Scripture study, and seek His presence more intentionally?

_____
_____
_____
_____
_____
_____
_____
_____
_____
_____
_____
_____
_____
_____
_____
_____
_____
_____

Consider joining a small group or Bible study to cultivate community and foster spiritual growth.

How can you actively seek opportunities for fellowship and accountability?

_____
_____
_____
_____
_____
_____
_____
_____
_____
_____
_____
_____
_____
_____
_____
_____
_____

Declaration

"I declare that I desire to grow closer to God in every area of my life. I will deepen my prayer life, engage in Scripture study, and seek His presence more intentionally. I am open to joining a small group or Bible study to cultivate community and foster spiritual growth. I actively seek opportunities for fellowship and accountability."

DAY 5

Cultivating a Healthy Routine

"There is a time for everything, and a season for every activity under the heavens.

Ecclesiastes 3:1 (NIV)

Reflect on your daily habits and routines.

How can you establish a balanced schedule that allows for rest, recreation, work, and time with God?

Identify one unhealthy habit you want to replace with a healthier alternative.

How can you sow the seeds of discipline and consistency in this area?

_____
_____
_____
_____
_____
_____
_____
_____
_____
_____
_____
_____
_____
_____
_____
_____
_____
_____

Declaration

"I declare that I will establish a balanced schedule that allows for rest, recreation, work, and time with God. I choose to prioritize self-care and create healthy habits that nourish my body, mind, and spirit. I sow the seeds of discipline and consistency, replacing unhealthy habits with healthier alternatives."

DAY 6

Growing in Emotional Intelligence

"A soft answer turns away wrath,
but a harsh word stirs up anger."

Proverbs 15:1 (NIV)

Reflect on the importance of understanding and managing your emotions in a healthy way.

How can you cultivate emotional intelligence by practicing self-awareness, empathy, and self-regulation?

_____
_____
_____
_____
_____
_____
_____
_____
_____
_____
_____
_____
_____
_____
_____
_____
_____
_____
_____

Consider seeking support from a trusted mentor or counselor to help navigate challenging emotions and cultivate emotional well-being.

Declaration

"I declare that I will cultivate emotional intelligence by practicing self-awareness, empathy, and self-regulation. I choose to understand and manage my emotions in a healthy way. I seek support from trusted mentors or counselors to navigate challenging emotions and cultivate emotional well-being."

DAY 7

Cultivating Authentic Faith Connections

" And let us consider how we may spur one another on toward love and good deeds, not giving up meeting together, as some are in the habit of doing, but encouraging one another—and all the more as you see the Day approaching.

Hebrews 10:24-25 (NIV)

Reflect on the significance of authentic relationships that encourage spiritual growth.

How can you invest in deepening your connections with other Christian women and fostering a community of support?

_____
_____
_____
_____
_____
_____
_____
_____
_____
_____
_____
_____
_____
_____
_____
_____
_____

Consider joining a prayer group or serving in a ministry to cultivate meaningful connections and grow together in faith.

WEEK 2
Planting Seeds of Connection:
Nurturing Relationships

"Friends are flowers in the garden of life."

a proverb

Sow purpose, growth, love's affection,
Emotions tended, faith's reflection.
Wisdom's bloom, gratitude and grace
Week two's journey, bonds embrace

DAY 8

Planting Seeds of Purpose

"For we are God's handiwork, created in Christ Jesus to do good works, which God prepared in advance for us to do."

Ephesians 2:10 (NIV)

Reflect on your unique gifts, talents, and passions. How can you use them to serve God and others?

_____
_____
_____
_____
_____
_____
_____
_____
_____
_____
_____
_____
_____
_____
_____
_____
_____

Identify one specific area or project where you can invest your time and talents to make a meaningful impact in the world.

Declaration:

"I declare that I am God's handiwork, created in Christ Jesus for a unique purpose. I recognize my gifts, talents, and passions. Today, I commit to using them to serve God and others. I identify a specific area where I can make a meaningful impact. I will plant seeds of purpose and watch them flourish in His grace."

DAY 9

Cultivating a Growth Mindset

"I can do all this through him who gives me strength."

Philippians 4:13 (NIV)

Reflect on the power of embracing a growth mindset, believing that with God's help, you can learn, grow, and overcome challenges. Identify one area where you tend to have a fixed mindset and challenge yourself to approach it with a growth mindset.

___

___

___

___

___

___

___

___

___

___

___

___

___

___

___

___

___

Declaration

"I declare that I have a growth mindset, believing that with God's help, I can learn, grow, and overcome challenges. I embrace new opportunities for personal and spiritual growth, trusting in God's guidance and provision."

DAY 10

Nurturing Relationships

"Above all, love each other deeply, because love covers over a multitude of sins.

Peter 4:8 (NIV)

Reflect on the importance of cultivating healthy relationships with family, friends, and community.

How can you invest in these relationships and nurture love, kindness, and support?

_____
_____
_____
_____
_____
_____
_____
_____
_____
_____
_____
_____
_____
_____
_____
_____
_____
_____

Reach out to someone you care about and express your appreciation and love for them.

Declaration

"I declare that I will cultivate healthy and loving relationships with my family, friends, and community. I invest in these relationships, nurturing love, kindness, and support. I am committed to fostering meaningful connections and being a source of encouragement and upliftment."

DAY 11
Tending to Emotional Well-being

"The Lord is close to the brokenhearted and saves those who are crushed in spirit."

Psalm 34:18 (NIV)

Reflect on your emotional well-being. What practices help you maintain emotional balance and resilience?

_____
_____
_____
_____
_____
_____
_____
_____
_____
_____
_____
_____
_____
_____
_____
_____
_____
_____

Identify one self-care activity that brings you joy and peace. Commit to incorporating it into your weekly routine.

Declaration

"I declare that I prioritize my emotional well-being. I engage in practices that maintain emotional balance and resilience. I choose to nurture self-care activities that bring me joy and peace. I allow God to heal and restore my emotions, finding comfort in His presence."

DAY 12

Watering Your Faith

"Let the word of Christ dwell in you richly, teaching and admonishing one another in all wisdom, singing psalms and hymns and spiritual songs, with thankfulness in your hearts to God."

Colossians 3:16

Reflect on the importance of regularly nourishing your faith through prayer, Scripture reading, and worship. Choose a Bible verse that speaks to your current season of life and meditate on its meaning.

How can you apply its truth to your daily life?

_____

_____

_____

_____

_____

_____

_____

_____

_____

_____

_____

_____

_____

_____

_____

_____

_____

Declaration

"I declare that I will nourish and water my faith daily. I commit to prayer, Scripture reading, and worship as vital sources of spiritual sustenance. I meditate on God's Word, allowing it to guide and strengthen my faith. I thirst for a deeper connection with God, seeking His presence with a longing heart."

DAY 13

Growing in Wisdom and Knowledge

"For the Lord gives wisdom; from his mouth come knowledge and understanding."

Proverbs 2:6

Reflect on the significance of seeking wisdom and knowledge through learning and personal growth.

Identify a topic or skill you would like to develop.

Research resources or classes that can help you cultivate knowledge in that area.

_____

_____

_____

_____

_____

_____

_____

_____

_____

_____

_____

_____

_____

_____

_____

_____

Declaration

"I declare that I am committed to growing in wisdom and knowledge. I embrace lifelong learning and personal growth. I seek wisdom from God's Word, and I am open to new insights and understanding. I invest in opportunities that expand my knowledge and equip me to serve others."

DAY 14

Cultivating a Grateful Heart

"Give thanks in all circumstances; for this is the will of God in Christ Jesus for you."

1 Thessalonians 5:18

Reflect on the blessings in your life and the goodness of God. How can you cultivate a heart of gratitude in all circumstances?

Write down three things you are grateful for today and express your gratitude to God in prayer.

Declaration

"I declare that I have a grateful heart, recognizing the blessings in my life and the goodness of God. I choose to cultivate gratitude in all circumstances, finding joy in the simple gifts of each day. I offer thanksgiving to God for His faithfulness and provision.

WEEK 3:
Opening the Garden Gate:
Establishing Boundaries for Growth

Healthy boundaries are not walls. They are gates and fences that allow you to enjoy the beauty of your own garden."

Lydia Hall

In the garden, boundaries bloom,
Vulnerability, freedom, joy consume.
Mindfulness sows seeds of grace,
Forgiveness whispers love's embrace.
Release control, let growth arise,
God's presence, our sacred prize.
Week three's journey, soul's delight,
Nurturing growth, in love's pure light

DAY 15

Embracing Vulnerability

"Therefore confess your sins to each other and pray for each other so that you may be healed. The prayer of a righteous person is powerful and effective."

James 5:16 (NIV)

Reflect on the importance of vulnerability in relationships and growth.

How can you embrace vulnerability and open yourself up to deeper connections with others?

_____
_____
_____
_____
_____
_____
_____
_____
_____
_____
_____
_____
_____
_____
_____

Write a journal entry exploring a recent experience where vulnerability played a role and how it impacted your well-being.

_____
_____
_____
_____
_____
_____
_____
_____
_____
_____
_____
_____
_____
_____
_____
_____
_____
_____
_____
_____

Declaration

"I declare that I will embrace vulnerability as a path to deeper connections and personal growth. I choose to let go of fear and perfectionism, allowing myself to be seen and known. I commit to cultivating authenticity and vulnerability in my relationships, trusting in God's love and acceptance."

DAY 16
Setting Healthy Boundaries

"Above all else, guard your heart,
for everything you do flows from it."

Proverbs 4:23 (NIV)

Reflect on the significance of setting healthy boundaries in your relationships and daily life.

What boundaries do you need to establish to protect your physical, mental, emotional, and spiritual well-being?

Write down three specific boundaries you will set and commit to implementing them in your life.

_____
_____
_____
_____
_____
_____
_____
_____
_____
_____
_____
_____
_____
_____
_____
_____
_____
_____
_____
_____

Declaration

"I declare that I will set and maintain healthy boundaries in my relationships and daily life. I recognize the importance of protecting my physical, emotional, and spiritual well-being. I choose to communicate my boundaries with love and respect, fostering healthy connections and honoring God in the process."

DAY 17

Cultivating Mindfulness

"Be still, and know that I am God.
I will be exalted among the nations;
I will be exalted in the earth!

Psalm 46:10

Reflect on the benefits of practicing mindfulness in your daily life.

How can you cultivate awareness of the present moment and bring more intentionality to your thoughts and actions?

_____
_____
_____
_____
_____
_____
_____
_____
_____
_____
_____
_____
_____
_____
_____
_____

Choose a simple activity (such as eating a meal or going for a walk) and practice it mindfully, paying attention to the details and sensations.

Declaration

"I declare that I will cultivate mindfulness and present-moment awareness. I choose to be fully present, savoring the beauty and blessings of each moment. I commit to embracing stillness, gratitude, and attentiveness to God's presence in my daily life."

DAY 18
Releasing Control

"Trust in the LORD with all your heart, and do not lean on your own understanding. In all your ways acknowledge him, and he will make straight your paths."

Proverbs 3:5-6 (NIV)

Reflect on the areas of your life where you tend to hold tightly to control.

How can you surrender these areas to God and trust His guidance and provision?

_____
_____
_____
_____
_____
_____
_____
_____
_____
_____
_____
_____
_____
_____
_____

Write a prayer that affirms your willingness to release control and embrace God's plan for your life.

_____

_____

_____

_____

_____

_____

_____

_____

_____

_____

_____

_____

_____

_____

_____

_____

_____

_____

Declaration

"I declare that I will release control and surrender to God's plan for my life. I recognize that God's ways are higher than my own, and His timing is perfect. I choose to trust in His guidance and provision, embracing freedom and peace that comes from surrendering to His will."

DAY 19

Cultivating Joy and Creativity

"You make known to me the path of life; in your presence, there is fullness of joy; at your right hand are pleasures forevermore."

Psalm 16:11 (NIV)

Reflect on the importance of joy and creativity in your life.

How can you cultivate more moments of joy and incorporate creativity into your daily routine?

_____
_____
_____
_____
_____
_____
_____
_____
_____
_____
_____
_____
_____
_____
_____
_____

Engage in a creative activity that brings you joy, such as painting, writing, or gardening, and reflect on how it nourishes your spirit.

Declaration

"I declare that I will cultivate joy and creativity in my life. I choose to engage in activities that bring me joy, inspire creativity, and reflect God's goodness. I commit to embracing my unique gifts and using them to bring beauty, joy, and impact to the world around me."

DAY 20
Practicing Forgiveness

"Be kind to one another, tenderhearted, forgiving one another, as God in Christ forgave you."

Ephesians 4:32 (NIV)

Reflect on the power of forgiveness in healing and restoring relationships. Is there anyone you need to forgive, including yourself?

How can you extend grace and forgiveness in your heart?

_____
_____
_____
_____
_____
_____
_____
_____
_____
_____
_____
_____
_____
_____
_____
_____
_____

Write a letter of forgiveness, whether to someone else or yourself, and release any burdens or resentments through the act of forgiveness.

Declaration

"I declare that I will practice forgiveness, extending grace and mercy towards others and myself. I release any bitterness, resentment, or judgment, knowing that forgiveness is a reflection of God's love and forgiveness towards me. I choose to cultivate a heart of forgiveness, experiencing freedom and restoration."

DAY 21
Stepping into Freedom

"So if the Son sets you free,
you will be free indeed."

John 8:36 (NIV)

Reflect on the freedom you have in Christ and the transformative power of His love and grace.

How can you fully embrace and walk in the freedom that is available to you?

_____
_____
_____
_____
_____
_____
_____
_____
_____
_____
_____
_____
_____
_____
_____
_____
_____

Write a manifesto of freedom, affirming your identity in Christ and committing to live a life filled with purpose, joy, and love. Take intentional steps to align your actions with this manifesto and embrace the freedom Christ offers.

Declaration

"I declare that I step into the freedom that is available in Christ. I am no longer bound by fear, shame, or self-doubt. I embrace my identity in Christ, walking confidently in His love, grace, and purpose for my life. I choose to live authentically and fully, impacting others with God's transformative love."

In the beginning,
Nourish temple, heart, and soul.
Clear emotions, spirit's seed,
In routines thrive, faith takes lead.
Embrace intelligence's art,
Week one's journey, faith's fresh start.

After the foundation is laid,
Sow purpose, growth, love's affection,
Emotions tended, faith's reflection.
Wisdom's bloom, gratitude, and grace
Week two's journey, bonds embrace

Then, watch, as,
In the garden, boundaries bloom,
Vulnerability, freedom, joy consume.
Mindfulness sows seeds of grace,
Forgiveness whispers love's embrace.
Release control, let growth arise,
God's presence, our sacred prize.
Week three's journey, soul's delight,
Nurturing growth, in love's pure light.

Until,
slowly,
yet suddenly,
all at once,

Amidst the blossoms, you find your way,
Transformation unfolds, day by day.
With heart aglow and spirit aligned,
Grow with Grace-
YOUR Life in Bloom;
your soul refined.

As we close the final pages of this transformative journey, remember that growth is a continuous process. Just as the seeds we've planted need ongoing care to flourish, your spiritual journey is an ongoing path of renewal. I encourage you to stay connected with the wonderful community we've built here.

.

About the Author

Phoenix Grace, host of the "Arise with Grace!: Stories of Women Moving from Pain to Promise" interview show is an emerging leader in the field of holistic empowerment for Christian women, specializing in faith-based wellness practices. With a Bachelor of Social Work degree, and a deep passion for empowering women, she has dedicated her life to helping women embrace their authentic selves, discover their unique identities in Christ, and achieve holistic well-being. Phoenix resides in Canada. When she's not engaged in writing and creating programs and products about faith-based holistic wellness, Phoenix enjoys going on nature walks, taking pictures of God's creation, and playing board / card games with her family.

live life IN FULL Bloom

Make your life a garden where you plant seeds of possibility and water them with *gratitude*

"Are you tired? Worn out? Burned out on religion?

Come to me.

Get away with me and you'll recover your life.

I'll show you how to take a real rest.

Walk with me and work with me—watch how I do it.

Learn the unforced rhythms of grace.

I won't lay anything heavy or ill-fitting on you.

Keep company with me

and you'll learn to live freely and lightly."

(Matthew 11:28 The Message)

www.lifeinbloomforyou.com

Subscribe to "Arise with Grace!," the podcast that celebrates and empowers the stories of strong, resilient Women of Faith who have moved from surviving to thriving and from pain to promise.

Thank you for choosing The Grow with Grace Journal—a part of the Inspirational Journals series. We hope you've enjoyed the experience.

There are many more journals coming, and we cannot wait to share them with you! To learn more about the Inspirational Journals series and get updates on our new releases, visit:

InspirationalJournalsProject.com

Share Your Feedback

If you could take a minute to review this journal on Amazon, that would be really awesome. :)

Do You Love The Idea of Creating Your Own Inspirational Journal?

Imagine having your own Inspirational Journal. Literally any topic can be leveraged and transformed into a beautiful journal format—and I'm here to help you walk through the process with ease. Inspirational Journals is a program for coaches, consultants, entrepreneurs, business professionals, ministry leaders, and other powerful people who want to use their experience and expertise to guide readers through a process of breakthrough and transformation in a key area of their lives.

Interested? visit

InspirationalJournalsProject.com for more details.

Manufactured by Amazon.ca
Bolton, ON